FIELD NOTES

Praise for FIELD NOTES

"Beautifully and interestingly written and thought-through, this collection of small, rectangular poems, like windows, weaves complexity into scraps of any field one might take into one's vision. A sort of desperation, an expanse, latent histories, memories, loves, harms: the field here is the space-in-which all these tensions coalesce, find various purchase, relations. Van Gogh, who killed himself in a wheatfield, CIA operations in America's 'strawberry fields,' the watched history of a family along suburbia's hems . . . 'a blue child of harm,' Cunningham writes, 'I fielded the destruction between them.' All is eerily troubled here: even the eye itself troubles the field 'of seclusion, isolation, estrangement, anomie.' Boys play war games in the field, graves appear, history goes on sown with seeds of threat. There is no absolution here, & if there is grace it is as sharp as a knife's edge." —CODY-ROSE CLEVIDENCE

"A treasure chest of literal and literary snapshots, Elizabeth G. Cunningham's *Field Notes* take(s) us, each one of us 'history's child,' along its polyvocal and polyvalent meanderings through fields of public and personal histories. Here, fields of childhood open onto the desire to flee from the figure of suburbia which longs also, from its shared post-pastoral condition, to return to some idealized childhood. Here a field is a field and is never only a field. Because it is haunted: the field of the page haunted by James Baldwin; the field of vision haunted by Vincent Van Gogh; *Strawberry Fields* haunted as much by international pop songs as by the spectre of Guantanamo and its neighbouring 'ghost detainees.'

"Through her delicate curation of inter-refractive meditations, Elizabeth brilliantly deploys ekphrasis to deconstruct the very act of looking. This book performs looking as a polysemous act: as the fantasy of objectivity, as seeking, as inherently political apprehension. Then, Elizabeth pushes this further. She reminds us that while the 'anti-god' of nostalgia might only return us to originary desire and its 'mystery memoir,' the perceiver is always the 'frame.' And that frame is in this picture. This beautiful epistemology of longing reminds us that looking is witnessing. I am grateful for this seditious weaponization of poetic utterance as ethos, as making, and as the urgent question of re-making." —ERINA HARRIS

"In *Field Notes*, Elizabeth Cunningham writes in microdoses that throw space open like sound amplified by a pinhole. Williams and Olson, among others, imagined poetry as fields of openness in the same way one might imagine a page with no print is blank, is silence: 'there's no hunting in suburbia.' Don't believe it. By some invisible folding of form into technique, *Field Notes* robs modern astonishment of this naiveté, this innocence, as if urging it, and so us, to grow up. 'Cause that page was never blank, that silence isn't quiet in the least—suburbia is a killing field. So Cunningham reimagines the field's openness as something the hunted dare not traverse, as something full of incipient destruction: a dry field isn't absent moisture; it's already ablaze. The photos that accompany the lyrical windows through which we gaze over Cunningham's remindfields kept reminding *me* of Rothko, who, like van Gogh, whom we meet in *Field Notes*, also bled out into his subject, an image of which there are no limited edition prints for sale. 'Childhood is a field in which we learn to construct fences,' Cunningham writes. *Field Notes* implies that writing—like growing up—means we mark where a few of those fences stood before they got blown away; then life is that thing we do in the crosshairs." —ED PAVLIĆ

E.G. CUNNINGHAM

RIVER RIVER BOOKS

Durham, North Carolina

FIELD NOTES

Published in the United States of America

Library of Congress Cataloging-in-Publication Data
Cunningham, E.G. 1985
Field Notes / E.G. Cunningham.
ISBN-13: 979-8-9881378-7-0
Subjects: LCSH: American Poetry, Photography, Visual Art.
LCGFT: Poetry.
Library of Congress Control Number: 2025933663

Cover photo by E.G. Cunningham
Cover and interior design by Alban Fischer

RIVER RIVER BOOKS
10 Linganore Place
Durham, NC 27707

www.RiverRiverBooks.org

The text is a limited field of possible constructions.

—Ricœur

FIELD NOTES

This field wants for nothing. This field is felt. Not by itself—as itself. Nearby is suburban blunting. There's no hunting in this field, not visibly. Weeds sprout. In wet season, its color is the child of blue and yellow. Its surface turns like swatches: pistachio, algae, emerald. This field is waiting. Watching, I think of matches.

In swatches, we drove past   open fields.
The night was felled   into wet horizon.
There's no hunting in suburbia,   not visibly.
An emerald want crept up in me from
                                                                  someplace
            wild. The felt harm of   not knowing. By
matches, memory's smoke went yellow
                                        and blunting. A constructed
process of finding out.

Mystery-memoir, call it *Field Days with Freud*. Mayday jubilee and folie à deux as he sits there smoking, some invisible historical anti-god of the field. I was six, and fell headfirst into the steel maypole. That expanse: blacked out, subsumed into previous years' unmemory, until a bell rang out.

Back then, our field was the ocean. Mother and father stood ankle-deep in open blue, turning in sun. Harvested flounder to place over fire later. I ran boundless and wanting only for eternity, on the edge of an awareness of felt harm.

This field is not so idyllic—a four-block stretch of land linked by suburbia and traffic—but that it exists at all feels miraculous. I observe it from the window: there it lies, framed by sunflowers and rotting fence posts, in swatches of beryl green and arid bronze. A flash of sky, a long road. I remember the opiate haze of childhood in patches. That absence does not rest peacefully. It sprouts like a latent seed in the field across from where I'm standing, writing placement.

A far-off field is felled   by boys with high-tech weapons. They start from home, singing a song about enemies, now played in airships over black fields at night. War is a blank name,   a lost season for history's child. Those fields hold their destructive futures like unlit matches. Every day, graves appear at the horizon line of blue and yellow.

Sunset peek-a-boo framed the cemetery field. I knelt. The grave: pitted and squirreled. The ground not there or no one is, the petals sick from display fluorescence. At the non-burial, I lay carnations, the felt silence as emergent as hunting.

A blue child of harm, I fielded the destruction
between them—*if you leave this house,* my father
said, *you're not coming back*—my sister on the stairs,
                    suitcase in hand. *Stop fighting,* I said.
                    First memory. The years between us
were battlefields of invisible want and invented
weapons.   *I won't,* she said, and didn't.

The new field was a horizon of blue, emerald, and yellow. We drove south with suitcases out of low country, the previous years' destruction gone buried. I felt myself turning. Childhood is a field in which we learn to construct fences.

Years of destruction. Summer and green. We grew older, rebellious, steely. Outdoor day drinking like we wanted to, like landlocked whales of grief, sweet and lonely, blunting our histories. Thought we knew art this way. Went cruel and wanting. An adopted process of blacking out. Residual fields cross back and cross over—

The girls pose in dresses amid yellow flowers. The field is trampled around them. I watch from the edge, silent and knowing, the childhood years swimming around them invisibly. Blue above and green below, their smiles are the suburban dream of want.

Auvers-sur-Oise, France, circa July 10, 1890, in a letter to brother Theo and sister-in-law Jo, Vincent van Gogh writes, "There—once back here I set to work again—the brush however almost falling from my hands and—knowing clearly what I wanted I've painted another three large canvases since then. They're immense stretches of wheatfields under turbulent skies, and I made a point of trying to express sadness, extreme loneliness."

I remember, on the edge of suburbia, a gated development called Elysium,

["Nothing remains but desire, and desire comes howling down Elysian Fields like a mistral . . ."]

built in the late 1970s / early '80s / lush, spacious lots / on Lake Champlain / oak trees / houses on a hill, houses below / a tended and tilled non-field / accessible by steep buy-in / and a belief in *keeping out*

James Baldwin, "The Artist's Struggle for Integrity," 1962:

You're in the position of someone on the edge of a field / and it's cold in the field / and there's a house over there / and there's a fire in the house, and food / and everything you need, everything you want / and you make all kinds of efforts to get into the house

and they would let you in / they would let you in, they're not being cruel / they recognize you, as you come to the door, that's all / and they can't let you in

you get in, let's say for five minutes / and you *can't* stay . . .

This field is a symbol of paradise. Captured in languid shots, filled with good-looking, pensive people. Erect a house to burn it down. Battle the locusts as they devour the wheat. In summer, I watch *Days of Heaven* across from that field now marked for a gas station. Across the ocean, for history's war, soldiers sang "Polyushka Polye"—little field, field—believing that space to be equivalent to escape.

Strawberry Fields (2003): a secret compound built near Guantanamo to hold "ghost detainees," so-called because of their hidden identities. The nickname, according to CIA officials, refers to the assumption that the detainees will be held there forever.

Strawberry Field (1936-2005): a Salvation Army-owned children's home and the inspiration for the Beatles' 1967 single "Strawberry Fields Forever," based on John Lennon's memory of playing within the home's grounds as a child.

Strawberry Fields (1985): the living memorial in Central Park dedicated to John Lennon following his murder in 1980.

Strawberry Fields (1997): an independent film by Rea Tajiri about a teenager's journey to the Japanese internment camp to which her grandfather had been forcibly removed.

A few miles away lies a field of fairground dirt, the site of the yearly county festival. In 1942, under Executive Order 9066, the fairgrounds operated as a "Civilian Assembly Center" in which Japanese Americans were held before transfer to more permanent internment camps. On its website, the National World War II Museum now offers a "Japanese American Experiences in WWII Electronic Field Trip."

The horizon is yellow. A dry season of blunted want. I watch the parched field, its uncolor like suburban ocean. Steel light bounces off the highway blur: cars pass like swatches of destruction. Early memories return like weapons:

pre-suburbia. Near an oceanic field, down dirt roads framed by green. We sat on the porch like a photograph of family. The summer was long and yellow. The old man looked through us, cruel and unnatural, lost in a blunted paranoia of harm. That man, my grandfather, turned visibly over the years. Emerged at the national horizon of folie à deux as a member of the Office of Strategic Services, whose

"Dogwood-Chain" was the largest U.S. intelligence-gathering tool of its time. I see him wild-eyed and bent over spilled mercurochrome, hear the sound of his slippered feet shuffling down the hall of history, I mean that house we stayed in—outside, we ate strawberries, bent our heads over someone else's harvest—inside, we blunted, did not say, for example, the words Central Intelligence. A child amid that foreshortened field of love, I lifted my head and watched the cornflower sky . . .

Slow wick burns over the timeline. Place shimmers. On a red clay afternoon, rural Georgia sears that *then* to now *this*. But I'm out west, where smoke drifts across blue and the yellow day broils, and I'm east, driving past tilled fields, arguing with a friend of a friend who works for Monsanto—GMOs, ethics, Haber-Bosch, history—to let the old husks drop and rot, and what of CO_2 and nitrogen, of famine and run-off—outside the window, a once-plentiful crop goes to drought.

Vincent writes, "I myself am quite absorbed in that immense plain with wheat fields as far as the hills, boundless as the ocean, delicate yellow, delicate soft green, the delicate purple of a tilled and weeded piece of ground, with the regular speckle of the green of flowering potato plants, everything under a sky of delicate tones of blue, white, pink and violet. I am in a mood of almost too much calm, just the mood needed for painting this."

Dogwood. A picket dream bloomed. Now we lived in suburbia. That nearby field was a grove: orange and emerald. My hands in the trees, their small white flowers. Night was a house of unknowing, wanting and invisible in early love. That wait: the futurization of history.

At the rumbling edge of destruction, Siegfried Sassoon writes, "the air was Elysian with early summer . . . I cannot think of it now without a sense of heartache, as if it contained something which I have never quite been able to discover."

I too discovered slantwise some delicate moment gone to murder. Felled any hope of escape and kept low, knowing any future destruction to be the cruel harvest of history.

At the edge of a mustard field, I watch and listen. Wait for the likeness to the previous years' love. Golden hour, a symphony of crickets, ephemeral spring. I prefer to conceive of the weeds as flowers. I am thinking of the word *delicate*, employed repeatedly by Vincent—and the unsteady step described in other letters, the "life . . . threatened at its very root."

Silent and wild, we blurred over the horse fields and made for the ocean. Night swam invisibly around us. Our love was urgent, turning under blue blankets. We held a horizon dream, hand in hand, of escaping suburbia.

The escape from suburbia was via history's fields. A childhood house went latent and invisible. Its green yard: a minor field framed by fences. Bells rang in wet season. To return meant doing battle with years. We took notes on love, made gods of want.

The paintings show the same fields in differing stages of green, blue, and yellow. A history unfolds in them, silent and emergent. I feel love in *Wheatfield under Thunder Clouds*, feel fluorescence in *Wheatfields at Auvers under Clouded Sky*, feel destruction in *Wheatfield with Crows*, whose brushstrokes resemble fences.

Those fields were no place for heartache.
Heat broke. In rainy season, still I thought of matches.

This field is pending. Weeds grow.

Surface rotates like samples of the moon under
microscope. The blue, budding desire to
discover what isn't. A low-lying
horizon of our last sharp breath. I felt
myself turn absent. And
waited for nothing good. Facts sprout

like weeds through memory. The past is a
fist or a flame threshing green. Silent and wild, we
blurred the

fields and headed for love, urgent, spinning under
blue years. We came out
steel and missing.

This field transforms looking to wanting. A horizon of silence and discovery. The previous years' destruction was folie à famille, hand in hand with a boy, wanting for forever. We swam in seaweed green and emerald blue, a humid fire at sunset. Those old harms knelt. Our escape was love. Our suitcases packed with ocean.

My mother applies oil to canvas in shades of grays and greenish browns, calls the painting "Forgotten Fields." I study the image of the photograph of the painting of that imagined place. An "immense calm," yes, and something else: latent and silent turbulence.

There is something supranatural about staring into fields. As one stares at the ocean, as the ocean is a field of wet blue, the act serves as evidence of seclusion, isolation, estrangement, anomie, a steely want left over from some internal destruction. Those wheatfield paintings were among Vincent's last. In late July 1890, he by all accounts wandered into his subject, the wheatfields, and shot himself.

"What is *up*," the poet writes, "with white poets and / meadows?"

Quoting Heriberto Yepéz, author of *Transnational Battle Field*, who writes, "There are no meadows in the mind of the oppressed" and "When sitting and feeling the wind coming / Through the trees / Outside I think / What is the relationship / Between the Poetry Foundation / & the CIA / Today? / The CIA shaped / The Writers' Workshops / That shaped you. / Is there a shape / Capable of thinking THIS / Without being a shape shaped / By the CIA? / The wind blows through the trees. / Poetry and the CIA have a history."

As a child, I thought the words I might put to the invisible weapons would be escape from that house, that hallway. Went headlong into history, blind as night, to arrive in cornfields, green as grass and unconnecting that *then* to the former's *this*. I raised my head to the crows circling overhead, that old man's death gone latent, our family scattered and fenced, and me gone exilic, hands over my mouth, wanting nothing but "nature."

I do not want to own the field. Nor walk through it. Nor pluck from itself any flower. Nor discard anything into itself. Nor leave any trace. The field is itself when I take nothing. Instead, I observe at arm's length. Know horizons this way.

That field is felled. By boys and matches. That field is wielded in a song about weapons, now played in airships over black fields at night. This night is a field of wanting, a felt season for a suburban child. A wet blue emerges like nothing hunted. For the previous years' harm, we knelt.

The field of want is never continuous. But extends forever. We learn through a process of turning, escape, and fences. Hold hands with the dry fire inside us. Know desire this way.

History is an emergent field that goes backwards and forwards. To escape requires love, a process of turning and knowing, of failure and feeling, wielding and adapting, forever. For a moment, out of history, we know no harm, stare into the boundless horizon, emerge vocal and immense into the night—

NOTES

all photographs, with the exception of that on pg. 35, were taken by the author.

epigraph, Paul Ricœur, "The Model of the Text: Meaningful Action Considered as Text." *New Literary History*, vol. 5, no. 1, 1973.

pgs. 26, 41, and 45, from Vincent van Gogh's letters to Theo van Gogh and Jo van Gogh-Bonger. Accessed through vangoghletters.org.

pg. 28, "Nothing remains but desire, and desire comes howling down Elysian Fields like a mistral . . ." from Walker Percy's *The Moviegoer*, 1961.

pg. 30, James Baldwin's "The Artist's Struggle for Integrity," from a 1962 speech to the Community Church in New York City.

pg. 32, see Terrence Malick's film *Days of Heaven* (1978), shot almost entirely at sunset in the Canadian ghost town of Whiskey Gap.

pg. 32, "Polyushka Polye," a 1930s Soviet song that translates, variously, to "Song of the Plains," "Meadowlands," or "Oh Fields, My Fields," narrated from the perspective of a Red Army recruit leaving home for battle.

pg. 34, Strawberry Field, from David Johnston's and Mark Mazzetti's "A Window into C.I.A.'s Embrace of Secret Jails," *The New York Times*, Aug. 12, 2009. The authors note, "The C.I.A. prisons would become one of the Bush administration's most extraordinary counterterrorism programs, but setting them up was fairly mundane."

pg. 35, "a few miles away" refers to the Merced County Fairgrounds in Merced, California.

pg. 36, aerial photograph (1942) of the aforementioned fairgrounds, then termed the "Merced Assembly Center." Creative Commons.

pg. 44, Siegfried Sassoon, "the air was Elysian with early summer," from *Memoirs of a Fox-Hunting Man* (1928), an autobiographical novel recognized for the protagonist's innocent frame of mind prior to the advent of the first World War.

pg. 61, "What is *up* with white poets and meadows?" and Yepéz's epigraph ("There are no meadows in the mind of the oppressed") are excerpted from Chris Nealon's poem "White Meadows," from Nealon's 2020 collection *The Shore.*

pg. 61, "When sitting and feeling the wind coming . . . ," Heriberto Yepéz, *Transnational Battle Field*, 2017.

E. G. CUNNINGHAM was born in South Carolina and grew up in Italy and Florida. She is the author of the full-length poetry collection *Ex Domestica* (C&R Press, 2017), and two chapbooks, *Apologetics* (FLP, 2017) and *Oranges for Venus* (Tilted House, 2024). Her work has appeared in *The Abandoned Playground*, *Colorado Review*, *The Gettysburg Review*, *The Nation*, *Poetry London*, *The Poetry Review*, *Puerto del Sol*, *Southern Humanities Review*, *ZYZZYVA*, and other publications.

RIVER RIVER BOOKS was founded by Amorak Huey and Han VanderHart in March 2022. Inspired by the idea that you cannot step in the same river twice, two poetry editors join together to publish (at least) two exceptional poetry titles a year, as well as the Plainwater Nonfiction Series.

Poetry Catalog

An Eye in Each Square, Lauren Camp, 2023
Bullet Points: A Lyric, Jennifer A Sutherland, 2023
Dear Memphis, Rachel Edelman, 2024
A Geography That Does Not Hurt Us, Carla Sofia Ferreira, 2024
Pastoral, 1994, Joe Wilkins 2025
Your Mother's Bear Gun, Corrie Williamson, 2025
Field Notes, E.G. Cunningham, 2025
Encounters for the Living and the Dead, Jameela F. Dallis, 2025
Antibody, Elane Kim, 2026
House of Myth and Necessity, Jennifer A Sutherland, 2026
Scythe, Elizabeth Sylvia, 2026
Fifty Mothers, Preeti Vangani, 2026
The Visible Field, Zoë Ryder White, 2026

Plainwater Nonfiction Series

There Is News Along the Ohio River, Beth Gilstrap, 2026
Backyard Alchemy, J.D. Ho, 2026